The Two Travellers

Retold and dramatised from the
Aesop's fable as a scripted play
for three readers.

Ellie Hallett

This story works well as simultaneous reading for groups of three as 'out loud' classroom reading.

The Two Travellers is also suitable as a stage performance.

Optional props and wardrobe:

- Storyteller: Smart clothes as for a reporter.
- Travellers 1 and 2:   Hiking gear, sunhat/wide-brimmed hat, walking boots.

Abbreviations:
S   Storyteller
T1   Traveller 1
T2   Traveller 2

Ways to read this story

- Don't rush! This helps you to say each word clearly.

- Think of yourselves as actors by adding lots of facial and vocal expression. Small gaps of silence also create dramatic energy. These techniques will bring the story to life.

- If you meet a new word, try to break it down and then say it again. If you have any problems, ask your teacher or a reading buddy.

- Don't be scared of unusual words. They will become your new best friends.
  (New words strengthen your general knowledge and enable you to become vocabulary-rich in your day-to-day life.)

S	Once upon a time there were two bushwalkers who happened to meet just before the track went through a dark forest.
T1	Hello there, stranger! My name's Charlie. Looks like you are travelling the same way as I am, so how about we walk together through the forest?

T2	And my name's Tom. Nice to meet you, Charlie! This track goes through bear country, so I'd enjoy some company.
S	And off they went, chatting together happily while they walked along at a steady pace.
T1	We are making good time, Charlie, but we are coming to the darkest part of the forest up ahead. I really hope we don't meet a grizzly!

T2	I agree. I'd like to get to the town on the other side of the forest before the sun sets. The sooner we're through here, the better!
S	The two travellers became quieter and they walked a little more quickly. They watched and listened for anything that moved.
T1	Hey! What's that? I'm sure I heard twigs breaking! Grizzlies are very cranky when they are just out of hibernation.

T2	And they are very hungry! A grizzly waking up after a winter sleep will be starving. I suggest we walk as quickly as possible.
S	As they walked along, the two travellers told each other bad-bear stories. Each story was worse than the one before.

Optional improvisations can go in here.

The two travellers and the storyteller *ad lib* some gruesome bear stories.

Note: *Ad lib* is the abbreviation for the Latin *ad libitum*, and means 'as the performer chooses'.

T1	*(in an extremely scared voice)*
	I hear bear sounds! Something is crashing through the bushes! We're in trouble, Tom.
T2	Don't move a muscle, Charlie! I saw movement over there. It's a grizzly all right. He's huge and he's coming straight this way!
S	Sure enough, a huge grizzly bear came bursting out of the bushes and charged straight towards the two travellers.

T1	*(in a terrified voice)*
	I'm out of here, straight up this tree. I don't want to be eaten by a grizzly. Sorry Charlie, but at times like this, it's every man for himself!
T2	Hey Tom! Where are you? Are you all right? Here – let me help you. I'll give you a leg-up! Oh no! I've slipped over. Ouch! My ankle hurts! **Oh!** I can't walk! Where are you, Tom?

S	Without a thought for his companion, Tom had climbed up into a nearby tree, and was safely out of the bear's reach.
T1	Thank goodness I am a quick thinker! Hmm. I hope Charlie has been able to get to safety.
T2	Help! Help! Oh no! I think I'm a gonna! That bear is coming closer, and – ouch – I think I've sprained my ankle. What else can go wrong?

S	*(said urgently and dramatically)* There was no time to escape the bear. All Charlie could do was lie on the ground and stay still, even though his ankle hurt a lot.
T1	What's Charlie doing? Why - the silly fellow's lying on the ground, perfectly still. I wonder why he's doing that!
T2	*(speaking in a loud stage whisper)* Oh-oh! I'm done for! All I can do is pretend I'm dead.

s So Charlie pretended to be dead. He hardly breathed. He closed his eyes and stayed very still.

1921 Felician Philipp

S	The grizzly sniffed at his feet. He sniffed at his shirt. And then, worst of all, he went right up close to Charlie's face!
T1	That grizzly is sniffing poor old Charlie all over, and now he is sniffing his hair! Poor chap!
T2	*(eyes closed and speaking as if he is thinking)* This is the worst moment of my life! Yikes! What a hot and hungry breath this grizzly has. I could do with some help.

S	The grizzly gave one last sniff at Charlie's face, and then suddenly he froze in fright. He'd smelt mosquito repellant, and it reminded him of a bad experience he'd had as a cub.
T1	How odd! The bear has stopped sniffing. And now he has wandered off back into the forest as if he has thought of something better to do. That Charlie fellow is not going to be eaten after all.

1926 Jack Orr

T2	I can't believe that the bear's loud sniffing has stopped! I'll wait a few minutes more and then open my eyes to see if the bear is waiting for me to wake up. Seems very quiet, though.
T1	Well – looks like it's safe for me to climb down. *(cheerfully)* How are you feeling, Tom, old lad?
T2	*(looking around with wide eyes)* Am I safe? Have I really escaped from being eaten by a grizzly?

S	Charlie got up slowly and carefully. He tested his ankle by walking a few painful steps.
T1	Today is your lucky day, Charlie. And even your ankle seems to have mended well.
T2	Yes, I think I'll be able to walk slowly to the town. But seems you were able to save yourself without any trouble.
S	And Tom felt a chill in the air that hadn't been there before.

T1	Oh my goodness! I did a very bad thing, Charlie, and I'm terribly sorry. I should not have left you in such danger.
T2	What's done is done and can't be undone, Tom.
S	But Tom was curious about what he had seen. There was something he wanted to know.
T1	I need to ask you a question, Charlie. It's about the bear and what he said to you.

T2	What he said to me?
	What do you mean, Tom?
S	Charlie couldn't quite understand, so he asked Tom for more information.
T1	Yes Charlie - I saw it with my own eyes. The grizzly sniffed you all over from your boots right up to your face. He then whispered something in your ear while you were lying there pretending to be dead.

T2	Whispered in my ear? Let me think for a moment. Ah yes, the bear was very near my face, and I know I was feeling very frightened. And to you it would have looked as if he was whispering in my ear.
S	But Tom thought that the bear had whispered a secret to Charlie while he had been sniffing his face. He wanted to know what this secret was.

T1	He went right up close to your ear as if he was telling you something important.
T2	*(thinking quickly)* Oh yes. I remember now. The grizzly gave me some very wise advice. He said that in future I should be much more careful when choosing a travelling companion.
S	And it was on that note that the two travellers parted company.

All	And the moral of this famous Aesop's fable is … Misfortune is the true test of friendship.

The Bear and Two Travellers An etching by Samuel Howitt 1810

The Readers' Theatre series by Ellie Hallett

These **Readers' Theatre** stories have a major advantage in that everyone has equal reading time. Best of all, they are theatrical, immediately engaging and entertaining. Ellie Hallett's unique play-in-rows format, developed and trialled with great success in her own classrooms, combines expressive oral reading, active listening, peer teaching, vocabulary building, visualisation, and best of all, enjoyment.

ISBN	Title	Author	Price	E-book Price	QTY
9781921016455	Goldilocks and The Three Bears	Hallett, Ellie	9.95	9.95	
9781925398045	Jack and the Beanstalk	Hallett, Ellie	9.95	9.95	
9781925398069	The Fox and the Goat	Hallett, Ellie	9.95	9.95	
9781925398076	The Gingerbread Man	Hallett, Ellie	9.95	9.95	
9781925398052	Little Red Riding Hood and the Five Senses	Hallett, Ellie	9.95	9.95	
9781925398083	The Town Mouse and the Country Mouse	Hallett, Ellie	9.95	9.95	
9781925398014	The Two Travellers	Hallett, Ellie	9.95	9.95	
9781925398007	The Enormous Turnip	Hallett, Ellie	9.95	9.95	
9781925398090	The Hare and the Tortoise	Hallett, Ellie	9.95	9.95	
9781925398106	The Wind and the Sun	Hallett, Ellie	9.95	9.95	
9781925398113	The Three Wishes	Hallett, Ellie	9.95	9.95	
9781921016554	The Man, the Boy and the Donkey	Hallett, Ellie	9.95	9.95	
9781925398120	The Fox and the Crow	Hallett, Ellie	9.95	9.95	
9781920824921	Who Will Bell the Cat?	Hallett, Ellie	9.95	9.95	
9781925398021	The Ugly Duckling	Hallett, Ellie	9.95	9.95	

KNOWLEDGE
BOOKS AND SOFTWARE
PUBLISHING

www.kbs.com.au

Readers' Theatre